Reclaiming
ORIGINAL
INNOCENCE

Other works in the Sacred Apology series
by Wayne Kealohi Powell

The Truth Dialog: Embracing the Unlimited Self

*The Sacred Apology: Healing Cherished Wounds
through Compassionate Self-Responsibility*

By Wayne Kealohi Powell and Patricia Lynn Miller

*Hawaiian Shamanistic Healing: Medicine Ways
to Cultivate the Aloha Spirit* (Llewellyn, 2018)

Visit the author's websites:

shamanicbodywork.com
waynepowellmusic.com
sacredapology.com
globalha.net

Reclaiming
ORIGINAL
INNOCENCE

The Way of Ho'oponopono

WAYNE KEALOHI POWELL

SACRED APOLOGY ∞ BOOK 1

First edition, 2024

Book design: Laura Berryhill
Cover design: Laura Berryhill

Excerpts from *Love without End: Jesus Speaks* used by permission from Glenda Green.
Excerpts from *The Radiance Sutras: 112 Gateways to the Yoga of Wonder & Delight* used by permission from Lorin Roche.

ISBN: 9798882673788

This work reflects the experiences of the author and is not intended to be prescriptive, nor an authority for medical or psychological advice. Should you require a doctor, always consult a licensed professional.

To all teachers and practitioners of peace:
To all who strive for conflict resolution without violence;
To all who live as a true reflection of divinity, with
kindness, gentleness, and forgiveness;
To all who came to create and experience heaven on
earth—and to all who are learning to make it so.

To all who seek a more effective way to forgive,
a higher path to walk as the light of love,
and the freedom to be who they already are,
love in a body.

Only love is real.

–A Course in Miracles

Contents

Preface

Why and How to Read This Series

Most people have experienced an emotional wound or two at some point in their life. Sometimes those emotional wounds become associated with physical complaints, and stuck emotional complexes become aches and pains—or simply nagging patterns—that won't go away in the body. The good news is, these "problems" can be processed to become possibilities: they can set us on a course of discovery of who we are and the freedom to be our best self in our life and relationships.

Whether we are a healer or a receiver of healing, the Sacred Apology series provides guidance and transparency about the nature of our odyssey of discovery. It explores our life journey, unlocking and activating our personal and spiritual potential through the healing process.

The Sacred Apology series is intended to be read in order, and readers who start with a volume other than the first are encouraged to seek out the remaining volumes, as each of the three volumes offers a unique perspective and different insights into the healing process.

Some concepts are presented in discrete form while others are gleaned through immersion in the flow of the material. Main topics and exercises appear in an ordered progression to gently reinforce and build on previously encountered knowledge and skills. For easy reference, exercises are listed within each chapter in the table of contents.

This series is written with love from the perspective of several traditions that hold dear the idea that there is one benevolent source from which we all, and all of life emanate. Its major influences include Self I-Dentity through Ho'oponopono, *A Course in Miracles* (ACIM), the original teachings of Jesus, and holistic spiritual science.

For more information on some fundamental components of the healing process, readers may enjoy referring to *Hawaiian Shamanistic Healing: Medicine Ways to Cultivate the Aloha Spirit* (Llewellyn, 2018) by this author—Wayne Kealohi Powell—with Patricia Lynn Miller.

Aloha, and happy reading.

Series Introduction

Understanding the Nature of a Healing Crisis: Healing as an Ongoing Journey

There comes a time in each of our lives when all that we think we know just isn't enough to get us through another day, when all the spiritual philosophy and training we've had isn't enough to overcome the chaos we're swimming in, when everything we've done before—that worked before—isn't working now. Instead, it actually holds us back from what we truly want to feel: whole, inspired, innocent, and free of the fear of being alone and not being enough.

For me, it felt like the passion that was driving my locomotive of desire had expired somehow. I came to an impasse and couldn't move forward. I saw clearly that all my attachments were holding me back from creating a new purpose for my life. As in childbirth, awakening and journeying through the birth canal can be a very intensely painful process. The empowered birthing mother is wise to breathe consciously through the most painful contractions, and then relax fully in between contractions to gather strength, back and forth, again and again, until an entirely new human being emerges. As a metaphor for self-renewal, *a whole new way of being emerges*. An ever-evolving, fully integrated, aware, personal–spiritual self arrives, beaming more primordial light into this world—illumination.

> *Full transformation requires from us that*
> *the will for radical change overcome our*
> *want and need for more of the same.*

Of course we know all this, but when it comes to truly living what we know we tend to back away from the discomfort of leaving our somewhat dysfunctional habits, thoughts, and behavior patterns behind. Could this be because we as humans are naturally driven towards pleasure, towards what is familiar, and away from pain or change? It may seem to our former self that a full transformation would cost way too much on every level of our life. Letting go isn't something we are trained in, and it doesn't always come easy to us. Life will take many people and things away from us, and yet through the grief we stubbornly cling to the past for a reference of who we are.

To start one's life over again takes a lot of courage. We may need to become shamelessly vulnerable and insecure, surrendering with blind faith to a source of power beyond our comprehension. When I reached this point, I had to trust that power to guide me through the darkest of times, allowing and blessing the grieving of the past, breathing myself through it into a new lifestream. I have reluctantly surrendered into this life-shattering death–rebirth process several times in this lifetime. It is always darkest and most painful right before the rebirth, when who-I'm-becoming begins to "crown" inside the cosmic birth canal. The me that was before is dying. In our weakest hour there's no reference for who we thought we were. We can only lay still in wonder about what form the new life may take. Then, all of a sudden, there's a strong pull-of-being from deep within, offering a spark of primordial light to usher us through the intense pressure of the expanding walls of the birth canal, out the other side, into the light, with a renewed purpose for living.

After our new self emerges the umbilical cord must be cut, totally unplugging the previous dependencies that held our life together. Every new lifetime (within this lifetime) has a clear beginning and a clear ending before the latest upgrade can fully engage its new abilities, with a greater capacity to serve the family of humanity with purpose and integrity.

These "lifestream upgrades" assist to cultivate a refinement-in-response to new challenges we will face. These challenges assist in promoting our soul's growth through a primal evolutionary process of maturing our capacity to love and be loved without conditions. A good analogy would be that when we get a new phone, our phone number remains the same yet the new phone's hardware and operating system have advanced capabilities. The new phone has the latest technology and new options for managing all our communications. There are many new features to learn about and more room for memory with so much creative potential. Welcome your new operating system, your new lifestream.

When leaving friends and family behind, the feeling of grief can be overwhelming sometimes. For me, the "laying down and dying" process is quite full-on and necessary, as I let go into the arms of a delicate, sacred, spiritual recalibration. It's as if I must allow the previous bonfire of my life that I built so meticulously, that was ablaze with passion, to completely die out. Then I can clean out the ashes before building a fresh new fire—a new life. Beginning again with dry leaves, dry kindling, and a few pieces of dry wood, divine fire—as personal passion—has a new creative expression.

A lifestream upgrade may appear as moving into a new place after a divorce; beginning a new job or career; starting a creative project or business that stimulates a burning passion for a creative expression; giving away old clothes; acquiring new clothes, or a different car or house; learning a new dance style, language, or musical instrument; or joining AA or a new exercise or study group of some kind, meeting new people and perhaps starting a new relationship. It could also involve letting go of a very lucrative income at a job we no longer have any passion for, in order to follow a more heartfelt career that nourishes our soul and serves humanity in a deeper, more harmonious and fulfilling way. In other words, we are letting go of old familiar habits, agendas, pathways, and people, and allowing our innermost being to advise us in creating a higher, more evolved version of our life with more purity of heart—one that is in alignment with who and what we are becoming.

Discovering or rediscovering who we really are is like finding a valuable treasure inside of us—or finally meeting our innermost being and falling deeply in love with our angelic nature as our new best friend. We didn't even know our own being was here for us, let alone that it was possible to have a "live-in" companion who will always love us unconditionally, within all circumstances. These are life's most precious and exciting times: growing through all the challenges into serendipity, synchronicity, and the joyous wonder of feeling totally in love with our whole self; witnessing, walking and talking as keen awareness; breathing in infinity with ecstatic wonder of the great mystery.

Mystics often say that we are born into each lifetime for a specific purpose that gives our life meaning, and that within each lifetime we are given specific gifts to fulfill our soul's purpose. Yet we tend to get caught up in living a life that we didn't seem to choose, a life that was chosen for us by our parents or by our teachers and preachers. How do we find out who or what we really are? We ask questions such as Who am I? What am I? To whom or to what do I belong? Why have I come here? What is my purpose for living, right now, in this moment? Who, what, why? What do I believe in that may be holding me back?

A spirit-guided inquiry such as a *truth dialog* has always worked for me to crack open these questions and let in some light. Finding honest answers through prayer and meditation that come from our deepest heart's longing will serve our highest and best interest. The truth dialog begs for core-splitting honesty to reveal and uncover the authenticity of our soul's magnificence and reboot its original blueprint for an inspired life filled with meaning and purpose. This activation brings fulfillment only through witnessing the pain and joy of all our choices here, from moment to moment, while allowing our innermost being to guide us.

The games of the unconscious mind are many. Most of them look socially playful and somewhat harmless—until they hurt us deeply by activating our cherished wounds, challenging our beliefs and social morality about what's right and wrong, acceptable and unacceptable. Greed and misuse of sexuality seem to be the major moral offenses of our time. Our moral boundaries were put in place to protect us. From a viewpoint of higher consciousness one might ask, protect us from what? From ourselves? From being hurt and hurting others? From feeling our own darkness so we won't project it onto others? From our aversions to what feels bad, and our cravings for what feels good? From our human foibles and mistakes? Or from discovering that we are actually love-in-a-human-body, and this comes with huge responsibility?

Our experience of good or bad is merely showing us our beliefs and our preferences manifesting consciously or unconsciously. Carefully witnessing how our programming affects our feelings will assist us in reclaiming our free will to seek healthier pathways for our precious energy to flow into our personal and spiritual evolution with more grace and less resistance.

Our thinking, calculating mind dwells on the past and the future while our sacred heart lives in direct vertical communion with the timeless being that dwells in every cell of our body. It harbors all the qualities that we attribute to divinity—it is a sacred portal through which we can engage and experience our immortality. This is what keeps the sacred heart pure. And this is why we "go vertical" to connect with divinity for meditation and for processing life's challenges. When we align vertically with spirit, spiritual law activates and responds, assisting us to delete the old painful narrative. What happens next often appears as a miracle—a flow of divine love cascading from just above our head down into all our bodies—goodness overflowing once again through all aspects of our life.

Serendipity and synchronicity have reappeared to create a whole new experience of life. Thank God.

Let me remind you that love is a state of being, not a feeling. Peace is not a feeling. Joy is not a feeling. These cherished feelings arise as "fruits of being," cultivated from living in harmony with spiritual law. Feeling deeply loved, peaceful, and joyful are states of being that we cultivate very consciously and carefully from being fully aware that God is always present, living within our chaotic mind and physical body. Pure consciousness is living with us, as us, and for us.

The experience of living in this new awareness or perception becomes the spiritual practice of constantly witnessing, accepting and modifying all chaotic thoughts, beliefs, and misunderstandings—the base metals—into gold and silver. Then we, as awareness, arrive on a higher perch, embodying a more being-filled experience, transforming the "doing" of mistakes into lessons learned, through the eyes of the angel that we are, witnessing our humanness.

I sincerely encourage you to muster the courage to navigate through the minefield of conditioning and unforgiven hurtful experiences in various relationships. A sacred apology just might be the holistic medicine you've been longing for to rebalance, recalibrate, and harmonize all your relationships, especially the one with your own primordial light. When body-mind and soul are in alignment with spirit, the heart opens wide and all becomes possible. Tears of joy will flow as our vulnerability becomes easier to manage through the grace of a blessed life consciously lived.

As we close our eyes and dive deep within, with profound tenderness, we find a quality of pure awareness that we long for and perhaps didn't know existed—within a quieted, still heart. Let's explore this delicate, gentled aspect of our heart together with a willing, open mind. Our heart knows the truth of our existence as infinity alive in every cell of our body. Let us begin an inquiry to transform our wounds into possibilities, honoring what habits need to die, mature, and evolve for us to upgrade our experience of life on earth—a life that awaits our welcome. As we devote ourselves to living our full potential as love in a body, this practice will shower us with infinite blessings of divine and human love, beyond all conditional limitations.

Welcome to the rest of your life.

May all beings be happy,
Wayne Powell, D.D.

Key Points

Reclaiming Original Innocence: The Way of Ho'oponopono

- *Original innocence, the foundational concept*
- *What needs to be healed; cherished wounds*
- *Primary tools for healing self and others: the spirit channel; understanding reality; going vertical*
- *Setting healing in motion: protocols and responsibilities for healing*
- *Exercises and protocols for attentive listening; the healing temple*

Healing our body and our mind is a journey that offers our soul more freedom and liberation from the challenges and confinement of living in a physical body. When healing becomes our spiritual path, our soul matures more gracefully. Healing is not a point of arrival, it is a journey.

The purpose of healing is to remove what's blocking the experience of love and health from flowing more freely in our life. When a healing session is shared with a skilled practitioner, that person will simply listen to what we bring and respond to the challenges we present with an open heart and a fresh idea of how to navigate our healing journey for the best possible outcome. Good healing practitioners are trained not to judge or counsel us. They are present to witness the healing process by listening carefully to what is being called into and out of form through the spirit channel.

In order to facilitate healing in another, we first do the work of healing ourself. We learn how to "go vertical," uplifting into the spirit channel and letting go of our cherished wounds. This book contains many discovery and skill-building exercises to help us in this process. Once we have a deep love for ourself and can truly embody our own innocence, other people in our presence will be able to realize their own innocence and see it in others. This is the best start to our healing journey: original innocence. When we look into someone's eyes—as innocence—we can see their soul.

1
Innocent Perception

In the quest for experiencing our "original innocence," first we must understand what it is and become familiar with how to reveal its authenticity. Innocent perception is the act of viewing the entire wonder of creation just as it is, without interpretation through any idea or belief about what is good or bad, or what we think something or someone is or should be. Innocent perception is seeing everyone as original innocence, which of course includes us, the seer. Innocent perception is the pure perception of our primordial light, looking down upon us from above.

For most of us, seeing this way takes a lot of practice because we are "hardwired" to judge everything and everyone through our limiting beliefs and judgment filters. But we are actually born into this 3-D world with innocent perception, because we enter this dimension as the embodiment of original innocence. Just look into a baby's eyes. Infinity is perceiving you, in wonder of who you are as a form of energy looking at them, also in wonder.

Becoming aware of every thought and feeling that we have and learning to just observe it without a reaction or any embellishment is not easy for most of us. I have said many times to students and clients, *"It's a no-fault Universe,"* to impress upon them that there's no one else to blame when *we* misinterpret reality, but it will always bring consequences when we do. Energy is simply interacting with energy and creating an effect within our filtered *perception* of reality. We judge what we see, and then feel our reaction through our belief filters.

In the original teachings of Jesus, we find a very clear explanation of what innocent perception is and how it can be achieved. In Glenda Green's book *Love Without End, Jesus Speaks*, Jesus reinterprets the Beatitudes for Glenda and shares his wisdom on innocent perception with us in the sixth blessing: *Blessed are the pure in heart for they shall see God.*

Jesus speaks,

In the eyes of God, who knows nothing of sin, you are nothing less than perfect. Which is why the very act of sin is merely separation from your Source. In the purity of your heart you are one with your Creator.

Glenda asks Jesus, "Then why do we not enter our heart more easily?"

Jesus speaks,

Because you do not see yourself as pure, perfect and innocent. Until you see yourself in this way, you will not enter the Sacred Chamber of the heart. As long as you try to carry all your unworthiness and mistakes in with you, you will stay on the threshold of your heart and not enter.

Through innocent perception, you may also perceive the presence of God in all existence. This is purity of perception. Through practicing this, you can be at peace with your life and see the beauty of what is before you. Everything was created in innocence. Behold this if you would see the face of God.

Judgement will separate you from this sacred space. Judgement is actually the only sin of which a pure and perfect child of God is capable. Judgement was the original sin, *and continual pursuit of it will keep you from the presence of your Creator.*

The critical recognition, which humankind most needs at this time, is that dualistic approach to living is no longer useful. Our oneness of spirit needs to be recognized and implemented through acceptance.

You don't need mental formulas through which to view life or to explain what you're doing. Just be here and perceive. relax and just be. The real basis for goodness is love, then observing innocently and honoring life through compassionate service, according to one's purpose.

These words touch me deeply as I allow them to pierce through my ordinary view of life. I realize that to embody "original innocence" I must find a way to see everyone, everything, and every event in life as neutral, having no meaning of its own. Then, the purity of what is before me can reveal itself, as itself, without alterations.

This of course is not so easy when I'm holding onto a strong feeling of judgment, guilt or shame towards myself for what I did to hurt someone; or what I feel someone else did to hurt me. When I tune into it, I can feel the emotional charge this judgment is holding for me; as the *need* to be right underlays it.

I have taught myself how to defuse the charge by "going vertical" and dissolving it consciously with a powerful intention to restore original innocence to my point of view. I open a shaft of divine light above me and begin breathing deeply into a sincere forgiveness prayer-meditation, allowing the Holy Spirit to alter my perception as I say, "I choose to see this differently."

Jesus states,

> *Innocent perception is the great revealer. Love reality with such clarity and depth that you have no need to use it falsely or misinterpret it to anyone. Love of reality is the core of honesty and the essence of innocent perception.*

Of course, these ideas and concepts do require consistent, disciplined, devoted practice to embody them fully and experience a substantial shift in our awareness and our quality of life. Learning to sincerely contemplate infinity every day helps a lot. Practicing non-judgment helps a lot. With a lot of relaxed-yet-focused attention and a strong will, we can develop the ability to become sensitive enough to *feel* the sublime high frequencies of love divine, which are anchored within our sacred heart and which permeate through infinity as the heartbeat of all creation.

The following exercises will help us begin the quest to reclaim our whole self and ultimately have a feeling experience of our own original innocence.

EXERCISE: Centering in the Sacred Heart
Contemplative meditation

Our sacred heart is an active portal through which we can engage and experience all the qualities that we attribute to divinity. It lives in direct vertical communion with the timeless being that dwells in every cell of our body.

> *To prepare:* Find a quiet place to sit where you can meditate. Clear your mental image screen. Breathe slowly and consciously, letting your mind relax open. Focus your attention on entering your sacred heart, which is located in the center of your chest, just to the right of your physical heart.
>
> *To engage:* As you deepen your breathing, allow your attention to drop like a stone into the vast lake of consciousness where distractions ripple away.

Relax completely any mental images of who you think you are. Imagine that the purest essence of you-as-light is waiting for you to arrive and settle into the radiant stillness. Become aware of the pure electromagnetic field you have entered as the one spirit of all created form. Open to the *feeling* of being embraced by infinity as pure, conscious awareness within your own sacred heart chamber.

With regular visits to this chamber of priceless wisdom, eventually you will find dimensions of specific intelligence which are ever guiding your life into pathways of right action. This practice is a fundamental tool for recalibrating and rejuvenating our alignment with source. Whenever we need comfort or reassurance, we can always go home to our sacred heart.

EXERCISE: Original Innocence
Contemplative meditation

To prepare: Find a quiet place to sit where you can meditate. Center yourself in your sacred heart, using the techniques from the previous exercise. Still your mind and relax open your sacred heart, breathing slowly and consciously. Clear your mental image screen.

To engage: Bring onto your mental image screen a happy little baby. Just quietly watch the baby gazing out into the world. Its eyes are wide open and taking in the wonder of perceiving all that it's drawn to focus on through its senses.

Now imagine that the baby begins to stare directly at you with eyes wide open. At first this will fill you with a bubbly joy. Then, after a few moments you realize the intensity is building inside you because this innocent gaze of empty, unprogrammed, pure cosmic consciousness is looking into you and looking right through you, searching for its own reflection of original innocence, which is the mirror image of your inner happy baby.

Now, change places with the baby and become this innocent happy baby, with no programming, no agenda, no judgment. You are now the presence of pure love in a body. Imprint this feeling very deeply into your biocomputer, your body-mind memory bank: the feeling of being pure cosmic consciousness gazing into the world in wonder.

We are born into this world as pure cosmic innocence. We will depart this world and return to being pure cosmic innocence. What happens in between is impermanent. So why do we make such a big deal out of being human? The pain shows us how fragile we are, so we reach for something more real, more permanent. And in the end, we finally recover and experience what we always knew: *ONLY LOVE IS REAL.*

2
Cherished Wounds

What is a cherished wound? It's a wound that we don't want anybody to touch because it hurts so damn much. Where does a cherished wound come from? When someone yells at us over and over again for doing or saying something they don't like...When someone hits us or abuses us sexually...When someone tells us constantly that we can't do something even though we know we *can* do it because we have a deeper knowing that we can do it...When someone has wounded or killed us with a blunt weapon in battle...When someone has abandoned us and left us on our own when we needed them most...When someone betrays us... When our lover tells us who they had sex with while we were at the gym... When our body holds onto the deep imprint of a serious accident. These deep wounds are often carried for years, sometimes lifetimes. Until they are processed fully they will remain unhealed and will continue to have a nagging effect on our life and many of our relationships.

Most of us will try to make the world a safer place for ourselves by avoiding the wound altogether, telling anyone who gets too close, "Don't do that," "don't say that," or "I don't wanna talk about it!" At other times, the deep imprint the wound has made in us may cause us to fight back. For example, we may be the child of parents who say, "Don't become a musician because you will starve. Get a real job." As a teenager we think, fuck them, I will show them. And we develop our talent to become the very best musician we can be. We may have little to eat at first but we don't give up. As our feelings of worthiness to "receive" increase, and then, finally, we prosper beyond anyone's imagination.

We all grow up in a family which shows us how to survive in this world one way or another. Everyone's childhood is different, yet the same. If we have siblings, there will be more dynamics involved in our relationship learning curve. The more siblings we have, the more opportunities to experience and discover ourself. Our parents carry what their parents carried, which is quite often a lot of unhealed wounds lurking underneath their ethical, religious and moral beliefs. Hopefully, we're all doing our best, consciously or unconsciously, to evolve the family bloodline that we inherited.

As we grow spiritually and pay closer attention to becoming an adult, we become more able to clear and clean a fair amount of the family leftovers: unforgiven, cherished wounds within our blood-family lineage. Of course, we experience and share our unresolved baggage beyond our blood family. We will encounter it everywhere with everyone we have a relationship with. Whether a shallow friendship or a new partner/lover, we will encounter an opportunity to uncover our most tender, delicately hidden, unhealed complexes, held in a safe deposit box within our psyche.

EXERCISE: Cherished Wounds
Journal work

Discover your own cherished wounds. (To do this exercise with others, please refer to Books 2 & 3 of this series.)

> *To prepare:* Sit in a comfortable, quiet place and bring a pen and paper or a journal. Relax your mind— best that you can—and approach yourself with reverence and respect to inquire about your hurtful wounds and scars. Take a few deep breaths and allow your body to relax into this process.
>
> Now recall the most hurtful relationships, one at a time and scan them for any feelings of jealousy, envy, betrayal, abandonment, abuse, manipulation, unworthiness or feeling put down by others. These are some of the signs of a buried cherish wound.

To engage: Write down what you come up with, even if you have processed it a million times already, just write it down. Then, take a deeper look into your childhood and notice when and how these hurtful imprints began, and write it down.

Now, give each relationship wound a number from 1–10 to determine its current emotional intensity (1 being the least and 10 being the most). Write the number down and date it as a reference. Later on, after you have processed the hurt thoroughly, you can acknowledge your good work as its process matures.

Was this wound created with a brother, a sister, a parent, a teacher, a lover, a preacher or a friend? Then notice how that same wound has carried through into other relationships. Write it in your journal.

Now, imagine that everyone in your experience is innocent because they played their part perfectly to bring these wounds of yours (and theirs) to the surface for healing.

Some of these tender bits inside have been there forever, far beyond our capacity to know how they got there. Chances are good that in other lifetimes we died a few very tragic deaths. These occurrences involved other souls who were with us when it happened. They may have killed us or held us as we took our last breath. We meet up again with these familiar souls in this lifetime to bring our unhealed past to a final conclusion. The law of polar opposites will eventually attract a healing scenario to these unhealed relations. It's much like a good TV series, with episodes and seasons over many lifetimes, with characters coming and going throughout the seasons.

Understanding all this might shed some light on a current situation we may be in with someone we love, a family member, or perhaps a very intense brief encounter that may have hit us hard and knocked us off balance with a strong sense of unmistakable familiarity or chemistry. A very deep wound, or imprint, often will travel from lifetime to lifetime until it is healed. I have worked this out with many clients over 25 years of practice and seen how these imprints may appear as a kind of possession. This discovery drove me to set out on a very personal, self-healing mission to uncover all such wounds in my heart and heal them once and for all, and then assist others to do the same.

The underlying experience of life is often determined by these ancient wounds buried deep within the psyche. They only surface when someone activates them in a relationship of some kind. We call these wounds "cherished" because they are the tender bits of memory being tightly held onto deep in the heart so that no one can see them or touch them—especially not us. Yet, relationship circumstances will occur for the purpose of drawing them out for healing. Sexual intimacy will eventually bring all our most cherished hurtful imprints to the surface, presenting us with a golden opportunity to become honest and vulnerable, trusting our lover to trigger us and reveal what needs healing.

EXERCISE: Understanding Intimacy

Explore your own beliefs and biases about spiritual intimacy and sexuality as described in the chapter.

> *To prepare:* Sit in a comfortable, quiet place and bring a pen and paper or a journal. Relax your mind— best that you can—and approach yourself with reverence and respect to inquire about your hurtful wounds and scars. Take a few deep breaths and allow your body to relax for this process.

> *To engage:* Write down what you believe about intimacy and what it's for.

> *Now, write down* who or where your beliefs came from.

> *Then, write down* how intimacy shows up, or doesn't show up, in your life.

> *Finally, write down* how these beliefs have affected your behavior with and towards others.

> *Now, write down* your beliefs about sexuality and where these beliefs came from.

Also write down any wounds you may carry regarding
your sexuality with partners.

And finally, write how you would like intimacy and
sexuality to appear in your life.

Spiritual Intimacy Heals

The intimacy that pure consciousness offers us will stimulate cherished wounds to come to the surface and reopen. In this regard, sex is a very potent activator of our deepest wounds. It naturally reveals our unhealed complexes. When opening our sexual energy consciously, with tender loving care, we can draw divine light into the hurtful imprints for healing. When practicing conscious lovemaking, divine love and human lust will merge within an intentional unified field, cultivating trust between two lovers, which can be extremely healing for everyone. When sex is just sex, it can be very confusing for our subconscious mind to manage. Such a high level of intimacy surging through all our pleasure centers in the absence of love can lead to feelings of unworthiness, and guilt and/or shame may follow, because we were taught that sex was only for procreation, not self-pleasure. This was "sinful."

When our primal nature integrates more completely with our angelic nature, this unity will bend polarities towards procreation activity beyond limitation. New planets, galaxies and solar systems are born within the merging of two souls becoming one unified extension of divine love's creation. This is how conscious lovemaking has the capacity to dissolve the darkest most hurtful wounds that block our worthiness, allowing us to experience a direct infusion of cosmic light through all our energy centers, creating new pathways of flow here on earth, as it is in heaven.

With unconscious sex our human insecurities will shadow our experience just before, during, and/or soon after an intense sexual encounter. We can sense the armor that is guarding our heart's unhealed places and wonder if we have chosen the right person to share our vulnerable, damaged inner child with. We may even wonder why we should get deeply involved sexually with someone if the relationship isn't going to actually heal our cherished wounds...do we really wanna go that deep down the rabbit hole with someone, knowing that it could take many years, decades, or even a child or two before substantial healing occurs?—if it occurs at all.

The daydream of a white picket fence, a warm hearth, good meals, gardens, kids, pets, a hard-working dad, and a nurturing mom who cooks and cleans all the time is planted pretty deeply within our psyche. It all seems so perfect until it crashes, over and over again. Using relationship as a comfort zone for our personal insecurities will always become a high-speed emotional rollercoaster and eventually derail itself. Finding security, permanence, and unconditional love in this world with another are the three human daydreams we must overcome in order to claim these qualities from our own being, from our divinity, to become sovereign.

We may be able to cruise for a while in a seemingly "normal" relationship, but when the sexual attraction wears off and complications set in, we may wonder if we still belong with this person. If we have children we most likely will stay as long as possible. But if we don't, we might just wander into another attraction and begin a new daydream all over again with someone else. We all know that the conscious choice would be to heal all that we can in the relationship we are currently in before moving on—a self-responsible, mature approach. It takes great courage to be so vulnerable with another. A lot of trust in our evolutionary process helps immensely in undergoing such an intense personal growth experience with someone else. To know that the one we have chosen to be with is with us for the purpose of healing and maturing is the best foundation for an intimate sexual relationship, or any relationship. Each of us claiming full responsibility for our thoughts, feelings and projections is what promotes healing to naturally unfold.

To be fully conscious in a life well lived, we must call out and heal the various wounds being reflected in all our relationships. As we do, over time we will become a "lighthouse" in service to divinity. Our family, our community, and our close friends will feel the softening and opening of our deeper heart. Everyone in our orbit will be touched in some way by the higher frequency shift within us as we walk through life.

> *Toward the One, the perfection of love,*
> *harmony and beauty.*
>
> –Sufi invocation

We are here to prosper in loving ways, healing all our cherished wounds. But before this can take place we must dig deep and clean out the basement of our psyche, which may feel quite painful to do sometimes. The process of elimination is how we earn the right to experience illumination. Eliminate what doesn't belong, what is not love within you, and you will prosper in ways beyond your imagination. Our sacred vision is at hand: the vision of everyone showing up consciously, in full integrity, each with unique gifts, whatever they are, and sharing those gifts selflessly. There's no greater fulfillment than to be kind and generous here on earth.

God held nothing back in creating this 3-D reality for us to learn and grow in. I feel so fortunate living in North America at this time, with clean drinking water, good food, shelter, and purposeful living. These blessings are for us to enjoy and share for the short time we are here. Let's take the best care of ourselves, Mother Earth, and each other, sharing these blessings whenever and wherever we can.

My prayer is that *all* beings here on earth have clean and healthy water to drink, food to eat, and suitable shelter from the natural elements. We have all the resources and technology that we need to accomplish this now. When the astronauts view the earth from the international space station, they weep with reverence, respect, and compassion because it is so obvious that we are one world-family: many countries, yet they see no borders, many peoples, but they see no separation. They see that we are united and yet our existence here is exceedingly fragile. They return to earth with a profound gratitude for life, an endearing respect for Mother Earth and all her inhabitants and the possibilities for a brighter future.

EXERCISE: Reclaiming Our Innocence
Journal work

Now ask yourself these questions in sequence. Feel into the answers and let what arises from your memory fully bloom in your vulnerable heart...

What is something that I did or said that I think I shouldn't have done or said?

What is something that I failed to do, that I think I should have done?

How do I think that affected myself and the others involved?

What would I do differently now?

Can I forgive myself for acting the way that I did?
Can I see and feel into my innocence now?

With honest vulnerability, feel deeply and answer these questions. This will clear the pathways that are blocking your abundance. Do this every day, when you feel it, and your synchronicities with life will multiply!

3
The Spirit Channel

Physical (Material) & Nonphysical (Spiritual) Reality

What is the *spirit channel*? It is like a TV station that offers us peace, joy, and love all the time. It is the vertical highway that we can travel to resolve all our problems from a higher perspective. Access is universal and always present for us to use whenever we need to. The pure light of consciousness resides in us as the *one spirit* within the spirit channel. It's like the sun, always shining upon us from above no matter what pickle we've gotten ourself into. Yet, the one spirit has no single body of its own. It lives in everything and everyone equally, offering profound love and support for all our choices. When the physical perishes, the one spirit turns back into itself and soon creates a new form of expressing itself, through the spirit channel.

In order to experience this world the spirit must be in a body. Everything we see, hear, touch, smell, and taste in this world accumulates "data" to be stored in a physical body. We believe that the body is real because of what we feel through our senses. And we believe what our senses tell us, that this reality is all there is to life on earth. Well, nothing could be further from the truth. This is a world of polarities. Without the one spirit integrating the material and spiritual, this world would simply not exist. The material and the spiritual have fully merged into each other to provide you with a platform to learn and understand how to be in this world and yet, not of it.

Our mind sees how the people we meet have physical bodies that look quite different from ours. This is the illusion of separation that allows us to have a relationship with an "other." Yet, in the spiritual dimension, there is no "other." All is one. All is the unseen, unsmelled, unheard, untouched, untasted reality governing all of physical life simultaneously. The nonphysical or spiritual dimension holds the entire physical reality in place through a vibratory frequency we often refer to as love, spirit or God.

Our spiritual existence is somewhat difficult to see with our physical eyes. It generates no sensory data because it is not from this world. Yet, this nonphysical dimension is every bit as real as the physical. The primary difference between the two is that everything physical is temporary—mortal, always changing, living, dying—and everything of the one spirit is permanent—changeless, immortal, no beginning, no end. The coexistence of these polarities is the paradox of life as spirit–matter.

The universal interaction of physical and psychic data is the catalyst that creates scenarios in the physical world for us to overcome, so that we may discover and learn how to use love and develop a deeper connection to and within the one spirit. The primordial light that birthed our soul and beats our heart is always showing up as our soul's radiance in a body. Our soul is a luminous immortal being on a journey of self-realization through a definitive connection to all that is. Through and with our being we can overcome any and all challenges in the 3-D world more easily, because our being is eternal. The end of suffering is at hand.

When called upon, our being, as the one spirit, literally lights the way for us to thrive in this physical world. Because our origin is infinity, it has no boundaries or limitations, it doesn't know death as we normally think of it. Its orientation is that of permanence, of everlasting immortal life, after life, after life —learning, growing, evolving and dying, releasing itself back into the one spirit after each physical incarnation and each intense feeling experience.

When we have a profound revelation and experience the feeling of being immortal, it takes our breath away and shakes our belief system to the core. This is because the feeling of love in its purest form is the feeling of divine light living in and through our physical sensations.

Cosmic immortal light belongs to us all. Just as we all belong to it. It provides our being with a body in order to experience its life in a body, on earth. It oversees, or witnesses, everything we do, say, feel, and experience without ever judging us. It is the cause of us being here, and it is this pure light within each of us that a simple heartfelt smile from a perfect stranger reveals.

Because all physical forms originate from the one spirit, we are all intimately connected through our being within and beyond this physical dimension. We all have equal access to becoming aware of the (nonphysical) spirit. We can learn how to merge within its presence for various purposes that will evolve our soul's journey. We can invoke its awareness and call to it anytime for assistance. We can actually use it for communicating with other beings because they too possess the same ray of divine light within them. This universal communication portal is the spirit channel. And the password to gain access into universal communication is: *go vertical!*

Practicing how to gain access within—utilizing the spirit channel—has many rewards, providing healing for each of us as well as promoting the healing of all humanity. When we utilize the spirit channel successfully, thriving within it may become a way of life for us. Long-distance healing, as well as personal and impersonal self-healing, are a few of the benefits of using the spirit channel to make inner changes that will also affect others in the 3-D world.

All that I'm sharing here is purely practical. We don't have to believe in God or believe in a savior to invoke the frequencies of heaven or goodness for self-healing or for the healing of another. Everyone has equal access to the spirit channel through the origin of their being. When our soul was gifted a form, our *soul cluster* came as a bundle: spirit-mind-body. We came to earth to discover or remember our divinity through communion within the one spirit. At the time of our soul's birth, we were gifted with eternal life in that very moment: it's one of the features in the bundle. We are all stardust, billion-year-old carbon, spinning in space on a beautiful blue planet, somewhere between where we're going and where we're coming from.

In chapters to come we will bounce through psychological potholes that may appear in the road, filling them in with suggestions for a smoother ride. Some of the ideas presented are quite basic, offering practical tools and protocols for healing. Other concepts help create and activate transformational portals for those who are ready to navigate into deeper water as a healing practitioner, to make a difference in people's lives. As we develop skills to assist clients, or ourself, in removing what does not belong, more people will seek us out for help and the ripple effect will create healing in whomever they touch.

EXERCISE: Engaging the Spirit Channel

Explore the spirit channel.

What are our preconceptions or biases?
How can we use our mind and sensations to open to or reach the spirit channel?
Are we comfortable going within?

To prepare: Turn off all phone and computer devices so as not to hear them while you focus deeper within. Find a quiet space to meditate. If you don't meditate, that's okay, you can fake it till you make it. Choose a comfortable position and close your eyes.

To engage: Once you are sitting comfortably, eyes closed, in your reverent space, begin a breathing pattern from above your head into your belly. Imagine that you are breathing in light from just above you into your belly.

Now think of your higher conscious self, or your ancestors, and keep breathing in light from above you. As you breathe think about being one with all of creation. Keep breathing this idea deeply into your body.

Once you feel a sense of your expanding self, see if you can feel your ancestors around you. Keep breathing in light from above and open to the possibility that you are connected to a prevailing source of power that is beyond comprehension, that you can feel in your body—beating your heart.

This source of power is infinitely intelligent, benevolent and loving. It's NOT in any single form we can identify with. Yet, it is in ALL forms as life itself. As you continue to breathe in light from above, see if you can feel the light as W~A~V~E~S of ENERGY that you can merge with mentally and physically, and ride them into a connection with anyone, anywhere, anytime.

You are now in the spirit channel. Much work can be done within this sacred realm.

Our bodies are an integration of matter and spirit, physical and nonphysical. These interdependent forms create our ability to be in a body and support our coexistence here on earth. We tend to give all of our attention to our physical world because it comes through our senses. We can feel it, smell it, taste it, see it and hear it. So, I ask you, how is it that we can feel something before it happens? Or someone before they call us or walk in the door? This is because the energy fields of everyone and everything interweave like ocean waves and exchange unseen frequencies that correspond and communicate with each other through what seems like empty space. Science has discovered that space is not empty, it is full of particle energy.

Horizontal (Finite) & Vertical (Infinite) Reality

All the stories we tell ourselves are from our memories and have no life of their own in this 3-D world. Yet they influence our life and our choices immensely. Hurtful memories, when triggered, can react like parasites feeding off our energy. They came from our experience and can play total havoc within our lives now until we let them go. These memories exist on a horizontal plane, only in *our* mind. Everyone involved with a situation will remember it differently. These memories have psychic weight, because they imprinted with a strong emotional content. So when we feel trigged they respond like gravity and draw our attention away from the present to relive the past in our mind with emotions. All memories are from earthly experiences which were often quite hurtful and will someday completely disappear when we physically die.

The good news is that everyone has access through the one spirit to a clear channel of energy that the ancients of every culture have used for all forms of manifestation—the spirit channel. Above and below are the dimensions of vertical reality—heaven and earth. When we view ourself from above looking down, from our angelic higher self, it's easy to see that everyone is innocent, regardless of what they have said or done. We are interacting humanly to trigger what needs healing in all our circumstances. This is why we came and how we grow.

The spirit–matter paradox of life manifests through each and every one of us. The spirit, or vertical, aspect of this paradox shows up as light descending into matter. When felt through our emotional and physical body, pure conscious light feels like warm, compassionate love moving through our body-mind complex. This is the most natural high we can experience on the physical plane. The juices of procreation are flowing with trillions of tiny particles of light floating through all our energy centers, lighting us up. This is why we like to "fall in love." It comes with a chemical rush and the capacity to see someone's childlike innocence and *feel* our own innocent child jumping up and down in gratitude for this radiant connection.

When we were born, our primordial light descended vertically into our crown center at the top of our head to provide us with life in human form. This light from above is pure and clear. It has no story, no weight, and holds no agenda for us. Its presence in and around us is simply to provide abundant energy for all our choices, without any judgment whatsoever. This pure, conscious light has intentionally gifted us with life on earth, and functions as the "infinite," unchangeable, immortal aspect of our trifold being. We call it spirit. It represents the vertical connection within the paradox, as light descending. It is without beginning and has no end. It exists out of time and space within a higher dimension for us to access through the spirit channel.

Our physical body-mind represents the "finite," ever-changing horizontal aspect of the paradox. Everything physical has a beginning and an end, like all the stories we tell ourselves that are filled with personal dramas and dreams. They exist in the physical world or horizontal plane. Their validity is reinforced every time we share them with another or repeat them within our own mind. Because these memories are rooted only in our mind, when we physically die they will also die.

What ascends with us when our being departs from the body is the radiance experiences of selfless love that we shared through random acts of kindness and generosity. It's much like a savings account that grows and matures through our innocent expressions of love. The accrued interest from these loving acts shows up when our soul enters the lifetime-review process after leaving the body while departing from earth.

From within the spirit-channel, our source of infinite wisdom can be accessed to pierce through the veil of the darker, more dense stories that we tell ourselves. Our relationships on earth carry imprints—memories of pleasure, pain, hurt, exaltation, and sometimes challenges that are difficult to fully process and let go. All these stories have weight or density and respond to a kind of psychic gravity. Our mind thinks: I feel, therefore I am. It's also true that I am, therefore I feel. What makes our life most challenging is that we identify with our stories as being who we are. Yet we are *not* our stories, we came here to live and learn through them. We are spiritual beings having a human experience within a growth process sponsored by life.

It is fact that none of our dramas or hurtful memories are permanent. According to *A Course in Miracles*, "What is real cannot be threatened, and what is unreal does not exist." Yet the emotional intensity of the drama provokes us into believing that the stories are real. They simply provide us with avenues of expressing emotions, so that we can glean the value of managing and processing our fears and explore letting go of having to be right. Our "pain-body" awakens and moves into "react" every time one of our hurtful memories is triggered by someone or something.

We have learned that the consequences of reacting from fear just creates more fear and more melodrama. Conversely, not reacting to our fear offers us a healing experience of being transparent, practicing acceptance for what is. The best way to restore harmony with others is to simply witness our emotions moving through our mind and body, and allow the pain to come and go, as it always does, without any resistance. Just witness and care for yourself through it. Everything on earth comes and goes. Tolerance is cultivated by being still within a storm fury.

Going Vertical

To go vertical is to make a conscious choice to fully embrace and then transcend our human experience through the spirit-channel. That's right—in the midst of complete chaos, or an emotional meltdown, or what may feel like a hurtful attack we can actually find peace within, and not react. We can merge consciously with our being, empowering ourself and witnessing the emotions that we feel instead of reacting to their intensity. Whenever we call upon divine light for assistance it will always bring a change in our human experience—lifting us into an upward spiral, altering our experience of conditional reality. This is why we dance, stretch, sing, chant, pray, and meditate: to align vertically with spirit and be showered with blessings of love divine.

The following verses from *The Radiance Sutras* best describe the soul's journey through our habits of chasing pleasure to avoid suffering—habits that often create more suffering in their wake. The sutras offer an awareness of spirit's navigation through the tendencies of our body-mind preferences, lifting us above the entrapment of clinging to our carnal nature into a universal oneness—a liberation of being.

Abandon these attitudes
Of wanting to prolong pleasure
And avoid suffering.
Let the heart be itself and feel
Whatever is there.

Free from clinging and avoiding
The heart regains its poise
And revels in creation.

Plunging deep into its center,
Discover that the heart is moved
By a pulse that is everywhere.
...

Consider all the pain and pleasure
You have ever experienced
As waves on a very deep ocean which you are.
From the depths, witness those waves,
Rolling along so bravely, always changing,
Beautiful in their self-sustaining power.

Marvel that once, you identified with
Only the surface of this ocean.
Now embrace waves, depths, undersea mountains,
Out to the farthest shore.

– The Radiance Sutras, vv 103 & 104, transl. Lorin Roche

EXERCISE: Go Vertical!

Imagine and/or experience horizontal reality as described in the chapter. What are the differences? Can you learn to witness yourself?

> *To prepare:* Turn off all phone and computer devices so as not to hear them while you focus within. Find a quiet space to meditate. If you don't meditate, that's okay, you can fake it till you make it. Choose a comfortable position and close your eyes.

> *To engage vertically:* Use your imagination, your will, and begin breathing in from above to access the spirit channel. What helps is to imagine God as an energy that you are in love with, and pour Her love into you as you fill yourself with gratitude for life and keep saying, "I love you," or, "I love us." This activates the spirit channel. The trinity of you—spirit-mind-body—is now engaged as one, within the unified field of all that is.

> *To engage horizontally:* We live in horizontal reality. Our mundane life as we experience it is filled with relationship challenges. We can easily feel the emotional weight that our seemingly bigger problems offer us to carry. Can you feel the difference contemplating how these problems make you feel from going vertical and connecting with your source of being?

You can teach yourself how to witness all horizontal behavior from a vertical point of view. When you do this, your stress level will plummet exponentially.

Practice this in everyday tasks, like washing the car or the dishes, changing your clothes, brushing your teeth or folding the laundry, watching your favorite TV drama. Observe yourself from just above you looking down on your actions and feel the impersonal nature of reality from this perspective. It's a very liberating practice! You will never feel alone again.

4
Clearing the Way for Healing

Navigating through Pain as a Facilitator

Navigating is a very useful concept in all healing work because we are always dealing with the unknown to some degree. For example, we don't know where our clients or their miracles will come from—they can simply appear out of nowhere. In this same way, when I'm traveling, I will be offered a temple space in some home or studio to do healing work.

As we show up fully committed to the healing process, we are offering an avenue of expression for the spirit of wholeness. When our heart is open wide enough to receive others into a healing temple, the laws of synchronicity and serendipity will fill our sails like wind across a calm ocean. As we acknowledge and invoke the elements and directions with prayer, they will flow into a willingness to guide us. This process is exciting and wonderful to witness: sharing another soul's healing journey is a sacred outreach for communion with infinity, cosmic divinity.

It's been said by many wise ones that pain is our greatest teacher. What people are usually seeking when they come for healing is help understanding, changing, or coping with some form of pain, emotional or physical. Yet, sometimes navigating through people's complex lives can be like walking through a minefield as an explosives expert, carefully stepping around the charges, disarming and delicately defusing each hurtful memory, one at a time. These "memory bombs," planted long ago during times of extreme hurt or trauma, have become reactive or even destructive behavioral responses when triggered. A few of them may even be from ancient wounds in lifetimes past. A soul's evolution is often facilitated through awakening and defusing these embedded imprints or memories when they become ripe for healing. Without intervention these imprints will persist, holding the opportunity for more suffering when triggered again.

As a client begins to open up, what's most important is that they feel safe, heard, and held in a loving embrace. Within this three-book series we will utilize some shamanistic principles and practices of deeper listening. These techniques, combined with a truth dialog and sacred apology, will offer a safe navigation for discharging hurtful memories. These tools will prepare us to assist a client in disarming their triggers, originally designed to protect them from further hurt, which are now embedded in the subconscious as volatile, reactive relationship patterns.

Become an Architect of Belief Systems

As a shamanic-style healer, it helps to imagine ourself as an architect of belief systems, a midwife of new realities. It is our responsibility to open ourself wide enough to learn how to spirit-navigate through the good, the bad, the ugly—all that may arise in the sacred healing space—with grace, while practicing full acceptance and thoroughly cleaning the recipient's story. We are never alone; we are always being given exactly what we need for healing when we call it in—praying it into form—before, during and after the session. Courage to facilitate someone's journey or take the next step through the memory minefield is always highly rewarded.

Fulfillment is assured as we navigate within vertical time—no time, timelessness—with spiritual guidance. We can do this, because it's not *we* who are doing it. After securely opening the spirit channel, we can learn to trust God and say what drops into our mind. We are receiving information from all around and within our client/receiver. To interpret it clearly, *we* must be clear. Then we and our receiver can open new pathways of being that promote an upward spiral.

Safety First

When a healer and a client/receiver agree to engage in a healing process, no healing can begin without first establishing a bond of trust. Trust is the foundation for healing to occur: trust in the healer's ability; trust in God's ability; and trust in the receiver's ability to open and let go of what doesn't belong, for them to become free of what is causing their suffering. When the receiver trusts the healer the forgiveness process will unfold more easily because the receiver feels safe enough to express innermost feelings they may not have shared with anyone before.

Trust is established when the healer receives and respects the client's beliefs, a process that begins immediately through inquiry. When the client hears the healer repeat what they have said—in their own words—they will feel that they are safe and truly heard. As their tender heart begins to open, they will trust the healer with the deeper, more intimate layers of their story. Sharing their feelings openly with the healer is a form of psychic detoxing for the client. This is the client's role within a dialog of core-splitting honesty—a truth dialog—to uproot the nagging memories that have sabotaged their energy and restricted their experience of peace with certain kinds of people who trigger them.

As the healer holds vertical alignment within themself, spirit will prompt specific questions to ask the receiver, questions that may lead to a thought complex or core belief that's holding the receiver's suffering or downward spiral in place. Once the wound has been uncovered, it can be unwound with compassionate acceptance, allowing divinity to guide the words, thoughts, and actions of the healer. Follow the gravity of love divine. Know that each moment is pregnant with a potential miracle. Embody *active compassionate listening* with a warm, open heart—this process is essential for gardening consciousness effectively.

There's a very ambient feeling of warm illumination in the sacred space when a miracle appears. It's like the welcome warmth of a radiant sun rising within and around where a baby has just been born. Illuminated stillness lingers in the afterglow of heaven descending here on earth. Infinity has made itself known once again, in this finite world.

EXERCISE: Nature's Beauty

Feeling and creating safety; holding vertical alignment using natural beauty as an anchor.

Find a quiet space to meditate. Now, using your breath, go vertical. Breathe slowly and deeply as you imagine your soul's light, which extends above you, pouring into your body from above. Use breathing up and down through your crown to hold this vertical alignment in place with your soul's light.

When you can feel this light pouring into you, call up a beautiful flower into your mental image screen. Observe all parts of the flower very carefully, one part at a time: each petal's shape, contour, and fold; observe the stamen and pistil and all the various color combinations of each part. Can you imagine what it smells like? Now, breathe in this beauty very deeply and *feel it* seduce you with its radiance.

Breathe the beauty into your whole body, into all your cells and organs, beginning with your heart center, radiating outward. Allow the flower's exquisite beauty to fully envelop you. Now, notice how safe and loved you feel in this reflection of nature's bountiful loving presence—here and now. She will always offer us her beauty when we become aware of it in each moment of each day. Seek beauty everywhere you go and it will appear for your pleasure!

The Pre-session Process and Interview

Whether the healer's primary modality is bodywork, massage therapy, counseling, or sharing deeper psychological work, a phone or video chat prior to the healing session can give us valuable insights into what's really going on and how to best approach it. This conversation is also the time to create the understanding that all healing is self-healing.

The client must assume full responsibility for their own healing process because the healer's ability to assist them is in good measure facilitated by the client's own willingness to cultivate a healing environment in themselves. For me, the talk/story interview is important because I want a potential client to know that I am not in the "massage business," I am in the art-of-transformation business, where healing is actualized primarily through empowering the client with a renewed, potent connection between their primordial light and their body's wisdom.

Healing begins during the receiver's first contact with the healer, either in person or by phone. The healer can get a sense of where the receiver is coming from by the words they use and can begin feeling into what that person needs to be able to open and let go of what's not working for them. I would suggest using the gentle-detective approach, repeating back to the receiver without any judgment what you have heard them say.

If the healer listens carefully they can gently encourage the receiver to have more compassion for themself, reflecting to them that they are *growing* through the resistance of something uncomfortable. The healer assures the receiver that once they accept and process the discomfort fully they will most likely feel a heavy weight has been lifted, and then they'll understand why the discomfort was necessary. Healing occurs through an honest inquiry, tracking down the pain so that the truth may reveal a tender compassion that opens inner space.

The healer is often in the role of leading the client toward becoming open to something they may have no reference for. This "something" could be frightening for them. Yet this something—through the process of opening—has the capacity to transform their entire life. Once healer-client trust is established and the receiver senses the aroma of freedom from suffering, they will do almost anything to have it, including becoming responsible for holding onto their hurtful memories, their destructive reactions, and their blaming projections onto others. Then the stage is set to utilize some potent forgiveness technology, like a plumber's helper unclogging a drain.

The healer can show the receiver how to create healthier thinking habits that will manifest what they really want, giving them examples of what victim thinking will produce for them and why. A miracle is simply a shift in perception from fear to love, from being a victim to being self-empowered. Do not take this simple truth for granted. A major shift in the receiver's external circumstances will always follow a major shift in their internal perception of their circumstances. Feeling okay within their discomfort is a very high-quality vibration that opens an avenue for healing to begin. As the receiver learns to witness their feelings and not react, they will observe their victim patterns while opening their heart to heal their most cherished wounds.

Once a willingness to accept their discomfort is understood as part of the healing process, self-affirming thought patterns can be initiated. As the healer is receiving their story fully with loving compassion, it's always good to acknowledge the receiver for reaching out for help. This is their first step toward recovery. Healing will begin immediately once the healer has had the opportunity to align with the receiver's particular set of circumstances and call on their ancestors for assistance.

Vibrational healing occurs through a frequency shift or potent trance. This is the specialty of a good mystic, shaman, or minister. For clients who are seeking a longer healing session and want to make a more permanent change in their life's circumstances, the healer may desire to offer a potent prayer-meditation by phone or video during the pre-session consultation prior to the healing session. Offering a prayer-meditation can help the receiver cultivate a delicate detachment from their looping story and facilitates a deeper letting go into the current of change that must flow for any healing to take place. Offering the client potent thought forms as prayer immediately directs their will toward the shift they want, empowering their process of letting go to live life in more peace.

I offer a prayer-meditation as a mantra at the end of the consultation in order to begin loosening the deeper roots within the client's hurtful story or self-inflicted drama. I will say to my client:

> *This prayer-meditation is most effective when repeated out loud, over and over, until you fall asleep repeating it. I suggest you keep it by the bedside until you memorize each line. This will assist you to engage with the light of your soul in setting in motion a powerful activation toward disarming the cherished wounds with forgiveness.*
>
> *Breathe each line in deeply after saying it. Repeat each line more than once, until you feel it going into the cells of your body. Then, do the next line. Say each word slowly, with intention to fully embody what you are saying.*
>
> *Once you have memorized each line, you can use any one of the lines throughout your day when you feel fear arising. Remember to go vertical and breathe in light as you repeat the mantra. Breath and light will empower the fact that you are love in a body!*

Prayer-Meditation to Prepare for Self-healing

I love myself deeply,
I forgive myself for everything,
I forgive all others for everything,
I trust and surrender to the light of my soul to guide
    me, protect me, and heal me—
Thank you, God, for this wonderful blessing.

Trances, Spells, and Belief Filters

Whether we are aware of it or not, we all live inside self-imposed trances or spells that act as thought-form bubbles, generated by our beliefs and assumptions about ourselves, about others, and about life. Whether we feel joyous or depressed, every mood is a trancelike state of mind producing an emotional environment that can often be influenced fairly easily with intention and minimal skill.

It's logical that our life experiences will be determined by our beliefs about how life works. From a shamanic perspective, the belief filters that were planted in our psyche long ago are being stored as truth. If we are in a deep trance of being sick, stuck, broken and afraid, depressed and angry, or feeling that we're not enough, we can create a shift into a different trance state that will change our current mood in any given moment into uplifting, life affirming feelings.

Once we recognize that we are being held hostage by a downward spiral trance, we can create a gestalt self-dialog, asking ourself questions about the specific thoughts that are holding our mood in place. Sometimes it helps to imagine that we are two people sharing different points of view, while examining and voicing out loud all sides, all perspectives of the mood we are experiencing. It's wise to assume a position that is delightfully detached, while watching and listening from above to the chaos or fear our mind is entertaining. Remember now, a miracle is merely a shift from fear to love. This can become one of our most cherished tools to master!

Judgment or Love

Only a complete acceptance of all that we are, and all that someone brings to us, will create a substantial shift in a receiver's beliefs and circumstances. In the safety of unconditional acceptance the receiver is able to open up to a higher truth that cannot be spoken, yet it can be abundantly felt within the healing space. It is a very high frequency of divine love. It is present in the healer's words and gestures, and also within the one that faces us, awaiting recognition.

The healer's humility allows the receiver's vulnerability a warm welcome, creating space for a healing trance that will overcome the receiver's story and activate a full letting-go of the unwanted charge that it holds. Then—shift happens! Spirit responds to our will, beliefs, and expectations about how wholeness is restored and regenerated. Just open into silence and allow transparency to unfold as the story is told and the receiver's tension unwinds. Just become love, attentively listening.

Listen carefully for what's *not* being said. Listen with an open heart, free of judgment. Do not identify with the receiver's story or it becomes your story. What the receiver really needs to begin their healing process is to feel heard, loved, and safe in the healer's tender care. The healer guides them, revealing through an intimate inquiry what their heart truly desires and who or what they will have to let go of, and/or become, to generate it, invoke it, and claim it for themselves.

To help anyone is really about loving *ourself* enough to be an agent of change for the spirit of unconditional love—overflowing from our heart into each person's heart who comes for healing. There is so much love in witnessing a receiver's meltdown within a delicate inquiry. As love for the person they have an issue with returns to them, they will be able to perceive that person's innocence. This experience is quite liberating for the healer as well as the receiver. It also releases the person the receiver thought was the problem.

Belief Creates Experience

Primary beliefs can range or shift from: "The world is a dangerous place" to "The world is a loving place"; "My dreams will never come true because I'm not good enough" to "All my dreams come true—I love and live them into being." Each one of these beliefs will elicit a very different behavior from the beholder and attract a very different experience of life. Our limiting belief filters— our blind spots—actually create the extreme challenges that keep showing up in all our relationships. Our assumptions about life stand firm as the structured fence posts holding up the barbed wire of our boundaries and deepest fears. These thought-forms will impose specific experiences from the limitations we place on our comfort zones and will reign over all our choices. Unconsciously, we will always choose comfort over discomfort, even when we know that an exhilarating adventurous life often begins where our comfort zone ends.

Managing Beliefs, Cultivating Safety and Trust

Our personal beliefs are our blind spots to a more universal spiritual truth or perspective. When we hold an assumption, a filter through which to see things, it creates a governing container for personal experience. People who believe the same things tend to hang out together. Where there is a mutual belief being held, the energy we refer to as love flows more freely. Ideas radically outside our belief-system may cause us to feel unsafe, insecure, and invalidated. When strong religious beliefs are challenged, people often feel threatened to the point of violence.

In ancient times a *kahuna* was trained to allow their beliefs to adjust in flux with each circumstance so that a wider range of possibilities could be accessed, unimpeded by any personal, limiting concepts the kahuna might hold dear. As miracle workers for divinity we cannot afford to be too attached to our personal beliefs about how healing takes place. Such attachment would greatly limit our effectiveness as facilitators for infinity. All we need to do is to set the stage properly, let go, and let divinity do the work.

When our beliefs are challenged, our need for control will kick in to protect us from feeling unsafe because our conditioned mind won't allow an experience that doesn't conform to how we think things should or should not be. Personal fear can only be softened by creating a feeling of safety in the midst of feeling vulnerable. For this reason, a healer should never challenge a receiver's beliefs with clever I-can-fix-it or I-know-what's-best mind schemes.

A healer can also do more damage than good if they allow any amount of rescuing into the healing process. Rescuing someone is not empowering them or helping them to heal. Nor is rescuing empowering for the healer. It's best if the healer sets their internal rescuer aside before, during, and after the session to simply watch—not participate. What we do is a "praying work" for divinity to manage the return of wholeness, perfection and innocence to the one before us. We are here for God as an agent of transformation. No rescuing allowed. It's unhealthy for everyone.

What's Good for the Healer Is Good for the Receiver

It's a good idea to examine our own core beliefs when doing our daily spiritual practice, just as when we assist others we inquire about their core beliefs in a truth dialog.

Regularly tracking our own core beliefs and working for their evolution enables us to better understand the looping patterns people find within themselves, and how to navigate them to break the loop more effectively. This holistic practice bridges the physical and psychological, as our physical experience is governed by our belief filters and assumptions about life. Our moral structures will play out in all our relationships, creating our experiences with others interacting with their beliefs.

Let's find out what we believe, or what we don't know about what we actually believe. The following exercise will help us begin a truth dialog with ourself.

EXERCISE: What Do I Believe?

Journal work

Ask yourself, right now, which of your beliefs are limiting you. Listen very carefully within. You may not have a clue about what your beliefs really are because they are buried so deeply in your subconscious. But write down anything you hear or sense and date it in your journal. You may be surprised at what being really honest will bring up in you. Most of us live in a fair amount of denial, all the time.

Examples: I believe that I'm ugly, or I believe that I'm beautiful. I believe that money is the root of all evil, or I believe money is a form of spiritual currency. I believe sex is only for procreation, or I believe sex is for us to experience heaven on earth. I believe in magic, or I don't believe in magic. I believe my spouse is an idiot, or I believe my spouse is a genius. I believe intimacy is spiritually healing, or I believe intimacy can be damaging and is only for making babies.

The above are only some examples. Dig deep! What do you believe?

Do this exercise as often you like. Tracking your deepest core beliefs makes it easy to see how your personal preferences change throughout your life as you grow through the stages of adolescence into adulthood, finally arriving into spiritual maturity, with the option to know yourself as pure and innocent, divine love in a body.

Can you see how your beliefs create judgments and hold you away from an innocent perception of yourself and others? Beliefs are imposed to create safety, yet they naturally create judgments, and where judgment resides, love cannot flow. So, list as many of your beliefs as you can find so that you can observe them carefully and begin to witness their effect on your life and all your relationships.

What we believe in becomes the pathway through which our healing will occur, either partial or fully. We need to feel safe to become vulnerable enough to open fully and heal. That is why it is wise to inquire into our own beliefs before we begin guiding someone else into a deeper awareness of what they believe. At best, we can guide them toward a higher perspective, one that originates just above their head, looking down on their life's circumstances. Having a client witness their personal drama as a movie, from above, is to empower them as an angel watching their life roles and the part everyone else plays in their movie. This offers them an impersonal detachment from the pain and pleasure they are experiencing within the melodrama—as an observer.

Privacy, Containment, Boundaries

When we become a practitioner of the healing arts, our life becomes divine love in action. If we want to enjoy long term success as a healing facilitator, it is essential to have healthy boundaries. Healthy boundaries grow out of personal values. As practitioners, we want to feel good at the end of the day about how we spent our energy. We learn to lovingly guide people through their choices and to practice forgiveness in a healing empowerment. Loving someone includes honoring their boundaries, and also, sometimes, challenging them. A belief filter may be holding up a boundary within their memories, causing their anger or hatred.

In sharing healing intimacy with others, over time, we become sensitive to the complex issues many carry around moral and societal boundaries. Taking full responsibility for our role as a facilitator of forgiveness means having healthy boundaries regarding our personal energy and our private life, and not leaking our sexuality. Respecting these protocols offers us greater success in working with a wider variety of people, and as *they* heal, they will send others to us for healing.

Speaking to a client about our personal life issues in order to have them feel more comfortable with *their* story will most often distract them from healing their own issues. Instead, they may try to offer advice on fixing ours. Remember, as facilitators of healing, we have a responsibility to help others rebuild wholeness, trust, and integrity within their personal lives. Therefore, we want to reflect and offer them wholeness and integrity from within our life. If we are leaking our energy, we can't help them to stop leaking theirs.

It's not uncommon for attractions to form while facilitating such deep, intimate healing work. In the context of a healing session, it is imperative that any chemistry arising in the temple remain purely heart-centered for the spirit of intervention to hold the highest frequency for a transformation. Acknowledge any primal sensations arising from your own body and simply draw them up into your sacred heart center, where you can love them with respect and compassion.

It's good to remember at all times that divinity is orchestrating the healing through us as we become a "hollow bone," or a bamboo flute that's being played by the spirit of wholeness and wellness for infinity. Your receiver will feel this moving in them as we breathe it into reality with each breath that we breathe for their healing. Also, it's most effective when we remind them often to breathe in light from above their head throughout the entire healing session.

For most people, sexual thoughts will distract them from their healing, leading them into familiar mental pathways of getting and sustaining pleasure, or rejecting it because of looping memories of sexual abuse. In a holistic healing session, we are focusing on a much higher-frequency band of energy than what we think of as "sexual energy." We are with the receiver to uncover their childhood wounds, allowing them to forgive and release any trauma being stored in their body-mind from all forms of psychic, physical, or sexual abuse and predatory harassment.

It is also important to respect the sanctity of a bond between two who were sexual partners, now separated or divorced, when one of them comes to you for healing. Do not engage in any melodrama or taking sides between the two. Our primary goal is to provide a safe haven or container for the receiver to feel loved and accepted, and express their feelings about what needs forgiving. In this regard it's very important to keep private and confidential the personal things that our clients tell us; we are forbidden to share their story with anyone. In honoring the containment of their time spent with us, their healing process will continue to evolve long after they leave the healing temple. It's also a good idea to practice *ho'oponopono* after they leave us so that their healing will continue to unfold without any projections forming or lingering.

The "God" Thing: Healing through Spirit

Since we rely on the power of spirit to create a miracle for us and for others, it is essential to acknowledge the source of all creation and call it into service for all manner of support and guidance. We may invoke out loud the spirit of healing whenever we feel prompted to through prayer, chant, mantra, affirmations, or song. Throughout the healing session, the presence of divinity will always respond to our invocation and be quite palpable in the healing space. This frequency is anchored with sacred intentions and a heartfelt gratitude for the process of life itself.

The healer can ask the client at the beginning of their healing session what they believe in or what they call the energy that beats their heart. It's good to know if the client has a reference for or belief in a spiritual power that they can call upon to assist them in times of emotional distress or challenge.

Enlightened master John de Ruiter used so many enjoyable, alternative choices for the word "God" in his public meditations. Some of my favorites among these substitutes are Gentleness, Tenderness, and Kindness. In fact many spiritual teachers, unless they are ministers, use alternatives for the word God quite often. If "God" is a trigger word for you or others, one suggestion is to refer to the divine as a verb instead of a noun, or use a descriptive charismatic quality such as gentleness, tenderness, or kindness. Many like to use universe, creator, or great spirit. Choosing our own alternative can be very empowering.

EXERCISE: Divinity and Me
Journal work

What are my personal conceptions of divinity?

Grab your journal or a piece of paper and a pen. Write down what you think God is, as a presence in your life. If you don't believe in God, then write down what you do believe in as the source of all life. Then, question your belief and write down what comes up.

Where did your belief come from?
Why is it so important for you to believe in, or not believe in a source of all life beyond our comprehension?
What is infinity to you?
Why is it important to contemplate infinity?
Are infinity and divinity similar concepts for you?

EXERCISE: Experiencing a Noun as a Verb

Turn all definitive nouns into verbs for a few days and see how that changes the energy within your mind, your heart and all around you! It will allow the energy of the noun to flow more freely as a verb than a fixed iconic figure or stationary symbol. Nouns tend to be rigid, and become more animated and powerful when utilized as verbs. They are more effective healing references as energy in motion (verbs), rather than as structured mental concepts or ideas (nouns).

A Clear Witness for Divinity

Being a good listener is invaluable in life for improving all our relationships. It is a wise and effective healing practice to cultivate attentive listening and not to respond to what's being shared until prompted by spirit from realms beyond what our senses can perceive. As a healer, we train to keep our heart wide open and relaxed, not fixing or protecting our receiver. Attentive listening on the part of the healer may be all that's required to crack open the vise-grip of a receiver's overly controlling mind, softening what holds a loop of habitual suffering in place. (Attentive listening training is expanded below and within Book 2 of this series.)

Healing always seems to be about releasing control or judgment of something—or someone—that's not working out the way we want. Whether it is anger, guilt, shame, or resentment that is being stubbornly held in the body-mind, it needs a potent dose of grace to begin to melt, break up, and flow downstream. It is very wise indeed to keep forgiveness on the healing menu. This offers us clear access to divinity as our partner in the healing journey.

Physical healing begins within the mental-emotional body. For a client's physical body to release something permanently, their emotional body must be onboard. Their inner child must open wide enough to allow what's buried as *undefined unforgiveness*, to heal. When a receiver "finds their way home," it creates an uplifting resonance of peace and praise that ripples through their family, their community, and the entire universe—truly a benevolent miracle.

By listening attentively when a receiver is sharing their difficult physical or emotional crisis, guidance is available to the healer in every moment as to what is most appropriate for the receiver to hear. The voices of the ancestors may speak to the receiver through the healer when invited. And there are many spirits unseen also listening with the healer who will offer guidance. When our mind is still and attentive enough, we can hear the promptings of ancestors, angels, and spirit guides ever so subtly, through intuitive feelings or sometimes as an internal visual image speaking to them through us. The rewards of being a very attentive listener are many. While applying healing techniques, a deeper opening flows through a deeper listening.

It is possible to listen through our hands, belly, feet, and most of all, through our feelings. When practicing the listening exercise during bodywork or breathwork, the healer will hear information from the receiver's energy field, and will know where to apply pressure and when to back off, as well as how far to take the receiver into the pain of an injury for a deeper release, or when to avoid using pressure in that area altogether. We can extract it, drawing it out of the body with shamanic techniques using the utmost compassion and forgiveness technology.

EXERCISE: Listening through the Body

To prepare: Go outside somewhere in nature where it is fairly quiet. Take your shoes off if you can and stand on the earth barefoot. Feet shoulder width apart, knees slightly bent, back straight. Open your crown center and look up with your inner vision—go vertical. Take a few deeper breaths from above you and allow your body to relax for this experience.

To engage: Close your eyes and open all your energy centers using your breath. Now, lift your hands up and extend them in front of you. Open your palms toward what's in front of you and pretend they are satellite dishes designed to receive transmissions.

In your imagination, pretend that your palms are now your ears, and listen carefully through your palms for what you can hear. Feel the energy coming into your hands as information.

Part two: With your eyes still closed, and all your energy centers open, place your attentive listening skills at the bottom of your feet. Open the palms of your feet and pretend they are octopus cups, designed to receive information from what they are attached to. Now in your imagination, place the listening skills of your ears in your feet, which are now your ears, and listen carefully through your feet for what information you can receive from the earth. Interpret the energy coming into your feet as information.

Key Protocols for Attentive Listening

The following summary of attentive listening protocols will be handy to reference here and as we proceed into the truth dialog and sacred apology processes in Books 2 and 3 of this series.

1. Go vertical!

Once we have established direct vertical access to primordial light—divinity—the spirit channel is open and ready to assist healer and receiver with grace descending. Breathe in light from above to envelop self and receiver in the power of God's presence.

2. Allow what is being said to be fully received into the consecrated space

The goal is a gentle, thorough inquiry toward letting go of what doesn't belong.

3. Refrain from sharing "woundology" with the receiver

Listen carefully to the receiver's story without identifying or agreeing. Do not share your own stories. Become transparent: let all story go through you as a transparent mirror, reflecting what the receiver has said without embellishment or judgment.

4. Verbally recognize the receiver's sharing

Part of attentive listening is offering that the receiver is fully heard and lovingly received. "Thank you"; "I understand"; "I hear you"; "thank you for sharing" are some phrases that clearly and simply acknowledge a recognition of the receiver's story.

5. Awareness brings healing, compassion, and greater understanding

Compassion channeled through the one spirit can radiate from the healer's heart center into the receiver's heart center and psyche. Inner listening can bring awareness of energies, ancestral patterns, and the unseen in the receiver's healing space, as well as unspoken truths.

6. Witness the receiver's body language

It contains information beyond the spoken story. Clues to guarded or hidden grievances may show up in facial expressions, emotional postures, or breathing patterns. Listen, reverently, openly, with a still mind. Allow emotions to fully bloom into the healing space to be cleansed.

7. Speak to the precious child within the receiver

No need to fix them. From a place of humility, reflect their soul's pure light back to them as they unravel the romantic or hurtful delusions they have imprisoned themselves in, only to discover that it's all really okay— we are all human and we are all forgiven.

8. To release the receiver's story, completely accept it as love listening

In the receiver's memory, the story is real. Loving acceptance reveals everyone's innocence, especially the receiver's own. With loving acceptance, reliving hurtful memories is like watching a good drama from just above the play. A higher perspective and loving acceptance brings release.

It is important to note that the body has its own wisdom and knows exactly what it needs for healing. It will only release something when it feels safe enough and is finally ready to do so—especially when the release is being managed through pain. Conscious, aware breathing is very effective for releasing stuck emotions; a potent circular-breathing session may be required to experience potent effective medicine.

EXERCISE: Judgment or Love?

Practice differentiating judgment and love while in the healing space; role-play both sides or work with a partner.

Part One

To practice this you will want to employ the attentive listening protocols from the section above, first with yourself, then with another.

As you speak, or as you think, listen carefully to the vibrational frequency of what you're thinking and saying.

If what you're thinking to say feels loving, it will glow a little and you will feel light expanding in you. If what you're thinking to say isn't loving, it will give you a feeling of confrontation with that person, place, or thing. This is judgment, contracting your energy.

Practice thinking various things and taking note of how they make you feel. If you perceive a more loving way, you may alter your experience of what you think, say, and feel from moment to moment, flipping judgment into its opposite, acceptance.

Part Two

Invite a friend to play this game. You can do it over the phone but it is better in person.

Ask the friend to speak about someone they have an issue with. After they vent a little, stop them and ask them how what they just said feels in their body. After they answer you, ask them if that's how they really want to feel about this person or situation. If not, ask them how they would like to feel about this person. After they answer you, ask whether they can perceive a more loving way. Then ask them how they feel after flipping their judgment into acceptance.

It's now their turn to inquire about your issue with someone to do this process again. Make it FUN! It's all about dissolving what doesn't belong, for more love to flow within and around you to and from all those with whom you relate. Loving someone feels better!

EXERCISE: A Sacred Space for Forgiveness

Creating a personal "inner healing chamber" for your forgiveness work. Healing is often about resolving concepts and beliefs that are not all-encompassing. We can forgive ourselves for holding these concepts for so long, limiting our experience of love and freedom.

Sit comfortably and go vertical. As you breathe golden-white light into yourself from above, allow a deeper relaxation to envelop you. Breathe so fully into your chest that your shoulders spread apart as they go back and your heart begins to open forward, spreading your ribs apart.

Now, create a chamber in your mind and label it "Healing Room." As you enter this room, take note of what you see. Begin to make any changes that you want, to offer a comfortable space for you to do your forgiveness work.

Now, address any issues that may arise as you occupy this sacred space. Use all the techniques in this book to absolve whatever is blocking a flow of creativity and loving innocence.

After you've completed your healing work, you may then enter your sacred heart—that part of you that is an anchor for your soul's light in a physical body. As you arrive into this sacred chamber, can you feel a clear, empty, holy space where you are completely innocent, filled with light, embraced by grace? Reside here for as long as it takes to bring a smile from your sacred heart onto your face, relaxed and joyful.

The Healing Temple

For both healer and receiver, the physical healing space is important enough to be created and cultivated as a temple. It is most easily cultivated as sacred space when we have a definitive connection with the unseen through the spirit channel. We may be advised to collect certain items from certain places, to adorn an altar with sacred objects from the elements and kingdoms of nature. Yet, less is more. A busy or visually "loud" temple space may distract a receiver from their healing. Stillness, quietude, reverence, warmth, and sparkling cleanliness are required for their busy mind to feel comfortable and relaxed.

EXERCISE: Temple Activation

Create your idealized healing temple, similar to exercises where people list the characteristics or qualities of their ideal partner, and activate it energetically within you.

Make a list of the qualities and characteristics that you want to employ in your physical healing temple, where you invite others for sacred healing.

After writing this list, look it over carefully and delete anything that's redundant or that would make the temple too busy energetically. I know this is a relative projection, but please keep in mind when designing a healing space that less is more. The less people have to focus on visually and energetically when they enter your space for healing, the better. (NOTE: People come with such busy minds for healing, we really want them to quiet their mind and relax their nervous system as much as possible.)

After you have fine-tuned your list, go vertical and activate the list within the cosmic realm where "all the perfect qualities and tools I desire are already present in my healing temple."

Now, say a prayer of gratitude toward your higher self, and finish it off with *"AND NOW, BY THE AUTHORITY OF MY SOUL, I CLAIM, IT IS DONE!"*

Appropriate Music Can Assist in Healing

When a client first enters the healer's clear temple space, their senses can play a very supportive role in their healing. Imagine coming into a comfortable and inviting place where a familiar aroma of incense lingers and the subtle sounds of soft music offer to the subconscious a safe and reverent healing environment. The safety and comfort of the space encourages the receiver's willingness to participate in their own healing. It sets up a potent frequency of recognition, allowing them to be aware that the Creator's presence is alive here and will be with them in every possible way for their healing. To that end, the perfect music mix can assist profoundly in a healing session, not only in setting the tone for the space but by establishing a healing trance that can pry open or melt a stubborn, armored heart.

As healer and receiver share a truth dialog or a sacred apology, the moment in which the receiver begins to speak their personal truth can be delicate. Sometimes the best idea is to have the room as quiet as possible. If background music makes it difficult to hear the receiver clearly or for the receiver to relax into the depth of a healing trance, then it is best to work in silence with only the natural sounds of the healing environment.

If prompted through the spirit channel to use music, music at a very low volume that is very tranquil may be soothing. Listening for spirit's prompting in every moment helps us abide in the flow of appropriateness before, during, and after the healing session. An inner voice may guide us in choosing what music to play, or whether a quiet, still space is best for the receiver's story to be told and for their memories to unfold and heal. Within a session, we may be pulled toward changing to a different music track that will better open the receiver or relax them more deeply. We can always respond quickly to find the right song or playlist by listening to our intuitive promptings and sense the receiver's energy moving in a new direction.

When the truth dialog and sacred apology are to be followed with some form of bodywork, the perfect music mix for the healer's and receiver's time together can greatly enhance the depth of any healing journey. For lomilomi massage, very gentle music for oiling the body can begin the relaxation process. In some sessions, the healer may be prompted to sing to the receiver during the massage, and can choose healing music that they enjoy humming or singing along with. If this is something you feel called to do, you can pre-create a few different playlists of comforting songs for singing along with. Many receivers love to be sung or hummed to. It gives them a sense of being loved as an innocent baby still in the womb, or a small infant in the arms of a loving parent or grandparent—and it can also be a profound mystical experience!

New Horizons

We have now laid a foundation, creating a temple of understanding that will honor the process of the truth dialog—revealing what needs forgiving—and lead us into a sacred apology, setting us free through forgiveness. Be brave and know that we are never alone in the healing of ourself or the one before us. There are legions of angels that support this miracle work because their joy-of-being is to lift our eyes above the horizon, to lift our spirits into the frequency of a gentle "okay-ness," and to help us reclaim our innocent perception of self and other.

Remember, we are here only to assist divinity to create perfect healing. We are present in the healing space to uncover the light, peace, and joy residing deep within each and every soul before us. These qualities often lie dormant until we remove what doesn't belong within the psyche and the body, to reveal the soul's human birthright, original innocence.

About the Author

Wayne Kealohi Powell is the founder of Hawaiian Shamanic Bodywork and Global Hoʻoponopono Alliance, a vehicle for extending the power of forgiveness worldwide. He is in service as a Doctor of Divinity, holistic health educator, applied kinesiologist, author, singer-songwriter, and recording artist. He has facilitated healing courses, private sessions, and concerts in Europe, the UK, Australia, and North America.

Wayne has studied Hawaiian esoteric shamanism since 1985 and began teaching kahuna science—huna and the way of aloha—on Molokai in 1995. His work honors the many teachers, students, and musicians who helped deepen his love for all things spiritual through four decades of exploring spiritual physiology and Hawaiian culture. He is the author, with Patricia Lynn Miller, of *Hawaiian Shamanistic Healing: Medicine Ways to Cultivate the Aloha Spirit* (Llewellyn, 2018).

As a teacher and through his books, songs, and prayers Wayne's passion is to assist others to reclaim their life's power and purpose. His courses and workshops can be found at shamanicbodywork.com and globalha.net. His original music can be found at waynepowellmusic.com.

Printed in Great Britain
by Amazon

41203689R10057